Living in
Bangladesh

Written by Ruth Thomson
Photographed by Jenny Matthews

FRANKLIN WATTS
LONDON • SYDNEY

This edition 2005

Franklin Watts
96 Leonard Street
London EC2A 4XD

Franklin Watts Australia
Level 17/207 Kent Street
Sydney NSW 2000

Copyright © Franklin Watts 2002, 2005

Series editor: Ruth Thomson
Series designer: Edward Kinsey
Additional photographs by Monirul Alam 23(br), Zahidul
Karim Salim 8(tl) and
Linda Trew 26(br)
Consultant: Linda Trew

A CIP catalogue record for this book is available from the
British Library.

ISBN 0 7496 6343 X

Printed in Malaysia

Contents

This is Bangladesh

Bangladesh is in southern Asia, bordered by India and Myanmar. Three large rivers, with hundreds of tributaries, flow through the country to the sea. These form the largest delta in the world. Most of the land is flat and less than 10 metres above sea level. The only hills are in the north and south-east. Tigers still roam the dense, swampy forest of the Sundarbans, in the south-west.

△**Tea growing**
Tea is grown on the hills around Sylhet. This area is cooler and has more rainfall than the rest of Bangladesh.

Fact Box

Capital: Dhaka
Population: 141 million
Official language: Bangla (Bengali)
Main religions: Islam (83%), Hinduism (16%), Buddhism and Christianity (1%)
Highest mountain: Keokradong (1,230 m)
Longest river: Surma-Meghna (669 km)
Biggest cities: Dhaka, Chittagong, Kulna, Rajshahi
Currency: taka

△**Memorial statues**
Bangladesh was once East Pakistan. These statues commemorate the founding of Bangladesh in 1971.

▷**Crops**
The soil is extremely rich. The main crop is rice. Others are jute, wheat and vegetables.

4

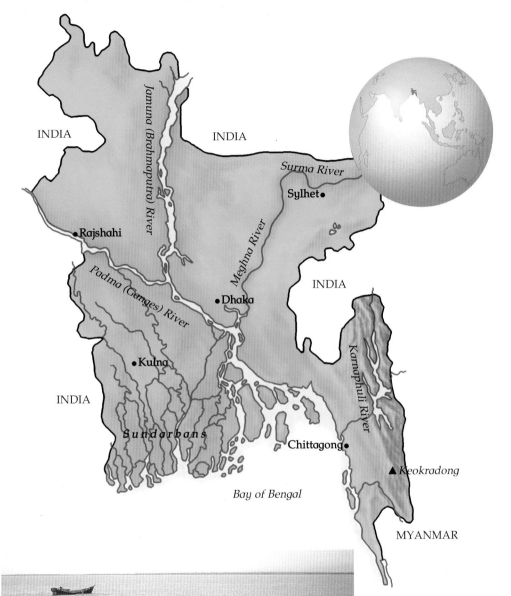

INDIA

INDIA

Jamuna (Brahmaputra) River

Surma River

Sylhet●

●Rajshahi

Meghna River

Padma (Ganges) River

●Dhaka

INDIA

●Kulna

Karnaphuli River

INDIA

S u n d a r b a n s

Chittagong●

▲*Keokradong*

Bay of Bengal

MYANMAR

◁**The coast**
The southern coastline
is almost 600 km long.
It is broken up by numerous
rivers flowing into the sea.

△**The population**
Bangladesh is
the most crowded
country in the
world.

5

A land of rivers

The Padma and Jamuna rivers that flow through Bangladesh start in the Himalaya mountains in India. In late spring, these rivers swell with melted snow and flood the land. This yearly event makes Bangladesh's soil rich and fertile. However, summer monsoon rains and cyclones can often turn the flooding into a disaster, washing away homes and crops and killing people.

△**Flooded land**
When the rivers flood, they dump a new layer of rich soil, called alluvium, on to the land.

▷**High rainfall**
More than 2,500 mm of rain falls each year. Most of it falls during the monsoon, between June and October.

△**Living by the sea**
People who live on the coast earn a living either fishing, harvesting salt or farming shrimps. They are most at risk from cyclones.

▷**A cyclone shelter**
Strong concrete shelters
are built high off the
ground. They keep
hundreds of people safe
during a fierce cyclone.

▽**Rice fields**
Raised banks of earth
surround the rice fields.
These trap water inside
the fields, so that the rice
can sprout underwater.

△**Water supplies**
Children enjoy the
plentiful water supplies
but they must be careful
after the monsoon as the
water is often polluted.

◁**Long-stalked rice**
Bangladeshis grow
long-stalked rice. The
grains ripen in the sun
above the floodwaters.

7

Religion

The star and crescent of Islam

More than four out of five Bangladeshis are Muslim. The rest are Hindu, Christian or Buddhist. Every community has a mosque, where Muslims pray together. Mosques have a prayer room and an area for washing. Often, there is also a *minaret* (tower), where a *muezzin* (crier) calls people to prayer five times a day.

△**At the mosque**
Friday is a holy day for Muslims. Men meet at the mosque for midday prayers and to hear a sermon. They leave their shoes at the door as a sign of respect.

◁**Prayer time**
This man is rolling out mats at a mosque, for people to kneel on when they pray.

△**Daily prayers**
Women and girls mainly pray
at home. They always face
in the direction of Mecca,
the birthplace of Muhammad.

△**A Hindu priest**
This is a Hindu
priest. He cares for
the temple where
Hindus go to make
offerings to images
of their gods.

◁**Ramadan**
During the holy month
of Ramadan, Muslims
do not eat or drink in
the day. At sundown
they break their fast
with something sweet.

△**The Qu'ran**
Muslim boys go to
mosques to learn to
read the Qu'ran (the
sacred book of Islam).
They cover their
heads with a *topee*.

Dhaka - the capital

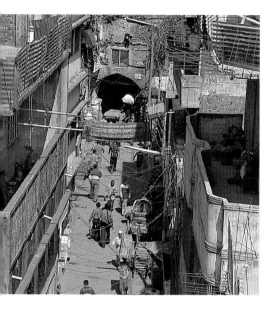

A view of a street in old Dhaka

Dhaka is the capital of Bangladesh and the biggest city in the country. It has two parts – an old and a new city. The old city is a maze of narrow, winding lanes with old houses and shops.
The new city has wide roads lined with modern flats and shops, high-rise offices, the university, several parks and the huge National Stadium.

△**The new city**
Most people in the new city live in flats, although there are also some houses with large gardens.

▷**On the river**
The river running through the city is always busy with ferries, cargo ships, tugs, rowing boats and motor boats.

◁ **National Assemby**
Members of Parliament meet in this modern concrete building.
It is built in the shape of a lotus flower.

△**City traffic**
The number of cars is increasing every year. There are long traffic jams, especially at rush hours.

▷**Air pollution**
The air is polluted with traffic fumes and brick dust from building sites. Traffic police wear masks for protection.

An internet café sign in the city centre

11

Living in cities

Fewer than one in seven Bangladeshis live in cities. However, the size of cities is growing, as thousands of people from the countryside arrive every year, hoping to find work. Most industries are in cities. There is a steel mill and oil refinery in Chittagong, which is also a busy port. More than a million people work in clothes factories in Dhaka or Chittagong.

△New housing
There is a building boom in high-rise flats. These will house better-off city dwellers.

△City jobs
Unskilled rural people may find work as labourers or as bicycle rickshaw drivers.

◁A shopping mall
In recent years, several air-conditioned shopping malls have been built in Dhaka.

△**Electricity supplies**
The demand for electricity is growing all the time. Cities cannot always supply enough, so there are often power cuts.

◁**Makeshift homes**
People arriving from the country cannot always afford city housing. Some make shelters on the street.

△**Baby taxis**
In order to reduce air pollution, new baby taxis run on clean, compressed natural gas (CNG).

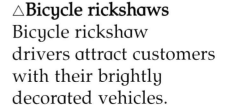

◁**Water pumps**
Those who do not have running water at home collect water from pumps in the street.

△**Bicycle rickshaws**
Bicycle rickshaw drivers attract customers with their brightly decorated vehicles.

Living in the country

Most Bangladeshis live in small villages in the countryside. Since almost all the land in Bangladesh is suitable for farming, villages are scattered throughout the country. People build their houses on the highest available land.

△**Village houses**
Houses are usually made of mud bricks, with thatched or corrugated iron roofs.

△**A water pump**
Tube wells provide clean water from deep underground.

▷**Walking**
Villagers rarely own cars. They may walk many kilometres a day, carrying heavy loads.

△A village shop
The village shop
sells basic goods,
such as soap,
matches and salt.

◁**A pot seller**
Travelling salesmen
walk from village
to village, selling
their goods.

▽**River fishing**
Villagers living
near rivers catch
fish in the early
morning before
tending their
crops.

Many villages are near a river.
Riverside houses are often built
on stilts. Mud embankments
protect homes and crops from
flooding. Irrigation canals
leading from rivers supply water
to fields during the dry season.

Working in the country

△**Tea picking**
Tea is an important crop. Workers pluck only the top two leaves from the sprigs of each bush.

▷**A tea factory**
Tea leaves are left to wither and then broken to release their juices. They are laid out to ferment and later dried. They turn dark brown or black.

Most people work on the land. Some have their own small plots. They grow rice, pulses and vegetables for their families. Wealthy landlords (*zamindars*) own most of the land. They pay landless people to plant and harvest their crops. Some landless people farm a *zamindar's* land and give him part of their harvest as rent.

△**Rice growing**
Farmers can grow two crops of rice a year. The main crop is planted in June and harvested in December.

△**A weaver**
In some areas, women set up wooden looms at home and weave their own cloth.

△**A goldsmith**
Skilled craftspeople work at home or in a workshop. This man makes gold jewellery.

△**Brick breaking**
Bangladesh has hardly any stone. People smash bricks into bits to use as hardcore.

Some of a farm's vegetable crops

Radishes

White pumpkin

Aubergines

Cauliflower

Beans

Green chillis

Red chillis

Some people earn money as craftsmen or labourers, or go abroad to work. People with neither skills nor land can find it difficult to feed their families. Organisations, such as the Grameen Bank, lend money to small groups of villagers, so they can work together to earn a living.

△**At the airport**
Many men with no land or job fly to the Middle East to work. They send money home.

Shopping

Shops are mainly small and run by a single shopkeeper. There are also traders who set up roadside stalls or wander about selling their goods. In cities, people can shop for clothes and household goods in markets, called *bazars*.

△**A food shop**
Only some foods are sold pre-packed. Shopkeepers measure out rice, pulses and other dry foods from large sacks.

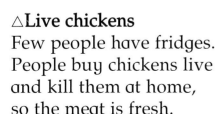

△**Live chickens**
Few people have fridges. People buy chickens live and kill them at home, so the meat is fresh.

◁**Neem sticks**
This man is selling neem sticks, which many people use for cleaning their teeth.

Bangladeshi bank notes and a stamp

▽A supermarket
There are a few supermarkets in Dhaka. Much of the food they sell is imported and expensive. Only the well-off shop here.

△Food shopping
People shop for fresh fruit and vegetables in open-air markets. Bangladesh recently banned the use of plastic bags. Now, people use shopping bags made of jute or paper instead.

△A bicycle shop
Bangladesh makes its own bicycles. These are a popular way to get about in such a flat country.

19

On the move

△A passenger ferry
Small ferries carry passengers up, down and across the bigger rivers.

△Lorry ferries
Big ferries transport lorries across wide rivers where there are no bridges.

In a country criss-crossed by more than 700 rivers, boats are far more important than road or rail transport. In the wet season, road journeys are particularly slow, as the heavy rain makes many roads very muddy.

A lorry painted with bright patterns and pictures

◁Buses
It is quite usual for passengers to travel on the roof of buses as well as inside.

△City transport
People travel around towns and cities in bicycle rickshaws, baby taxis or buses.

△Carrying the harvest home
After the harvest, farmers carry their crops home on poles, slung across their shoulder, like this.

Men carrying their shopping home from market

▷Delivering goods
Lorries are banned from Dhaka during the day. Goods are delivered on carts pulled by hand or bike.

Family life

Most people live in close-knit, extended families. When a woman marries, she moves in with her husband's family. This might include his parents, his brothers and their wives. Women rarely used to work outside the home, but this is now changing, especially in cities.

△ **Tribal family**
There are about 20 different tribal groups in Bangladesh. Each has its own distinct customs, beliefs and way of life.

△ **Family roles**
Women often marry at a young age. They generally stay at home, preparing food and caring for children.

▷ **Family size**
The average number of children per family has dropped from 6 to 3 in the last 30 years. Families are bigger in the country than in cities.

A father taking his daughter to school

22

Family life

△Wood collecting
It is often the children's task to collect wood for cooking fuel.

▽Child care
Older girls look after their younger brothers and sisters.

△Selling in the street
Boys sell snacks, drinks and flowers in the street.

In most families in Bangladesh, it is essential for children to help out. In towns and cities, boys often earn money to help improve the family income. In the country, boys help in the rice fields or tend the farm animals. Girls help with cooking and cleaning chores at home.

△Stone breaking
In some families, children help with their parents' job, such as stone breaking.

23

Time to eat

Rice, pulses and vegetables are the staple foods for most Bangladeshis. A typical everyday meal at home consists of boiled rice with spicy lentils and a meat or vegetable curry (*masala*).

Roadside food stalls sell cheap, filling snacks and drinks, such as sweet, milky tea (*chai*) and fresh coconut milk.

A selection of fresh vegetables in a market

▷**A restaurant meal**
A restaurant meal usually consists of several dishes served in separate small metal bowls. Other typical dishes include roti bread and chicken khorma.

△**Fish**
Fresh fish is cheap and forms a main part of many people's everyday diet, as fish curry.

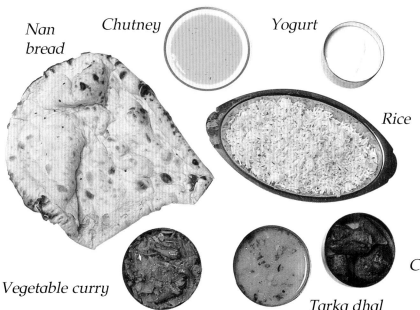

Nan bread

Chutney

Yogurt

Rice

Vegetable curry

Tarka dhal

Chicken tikka

Pan, a mouth freshener, is eaten at the end of a meal.

△Fast food
Western-style fast
food restaurants
have recently
opened in Dhaka.

△Snacks
Popular snacks include freshly-cooked hot
dishes, breads and pastries.

▷*Tiffin* delivery
Many women make
lunch for their
husbands. They put
the food in a stack of
metal containers,
called a *tiffin*. Boys
deliver the *tiffins* to
the men's workplace.

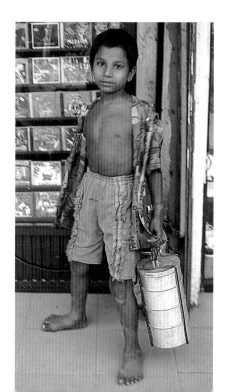

School time

△**A school bus**
Some children travel to school in a bus pulled by a bicycle.

Bangladeshis value education, but not everyone has the chance to go to school. Government primary schools are free and open to all children. However, poor families find it hard to survive without their children working. So, only seven out of ten children start primary school, mostly boys. Children usually go to school for three or four hours a day, except Fridays.

△**A private nursery**
Well-off families can send their children, from the age of three, to fee-paying nurseries.

△**A tea estate school**
Tea estates have their own schools, which children of tea workers attend.

△**A government school**
The government provides books and equipment for children in primary schools.

◁Secondary school

Boys and girls go to separate
secondary schools,
which are found
only in cities
and towns.

*School
books*

△Literacy

Only half the men and a third of
women in Bangladesh can read
and write. The most
highly educated group are
middle-class boys.

▷Higher education

Bangladesh has more than 15
universities and colleges. Dhaka
University, founded in 1921, is
the oldest.

27

Having fun

Weddings and festivals (*melas*) are colourful events that everyone enjoys. Some of the festivals mark the start of a new season, when people cook particular dishes and wear new clothes. Everyday fun includes swimming in rivers and playing cricket and board games.

△*Karam*
These children are playing *Karam*, a board game where players have to skilfully flick counters.

▷Cricket
Cricket is a popular sport. The national team competes in international events. Only men go to watch the matches.

△Chess
Players often set up a game of chess in the street. A group of spectators may eagerly follow it.

△In the park
The bigger cities have parks where people come to stroll and picnic. The parks often have boating lakes.

▷Satellite TV
The most popular programmes on TV are Indian films and cricket matches.

△A country funfair
Travelling fairs, with rides like this one, visit even the remotest villages.

Going further

The royal Bengal tiger

About 400 large tigers are believed to live in the dense forests of the Sundarbans, in south-west Bangladesh.

Find out about the life and habits of these tigers (see www.enchantedlearning.com or www.5tigers.org). Create a tiger-face shaped booklet about the tigers.

Rickshaw art

Bicycle rickshaws are decorated all over with brightly coloured designs. Painters include eye-catching images of movie stars, sunsets over dreamy landscapes and scenes of modern life.

Imagine you have been asked to decorate a rickshaw. Design a bold and colourful Bangladeshi scene for it.

Embroidery

In parts of Bangladesh it is a tradition for women to make embroidered quilts (*nakshi kantha*) for their children. These used to be made from layers of worn-out clothes, stitched together with patterns and pictures. Some are now made of cotton.

Invent your own quilt design, using dotted lines, like these embroidery stitches.

Websites

www.virtualbangladesh.com
www.greenbangla.com

Glossary

Border The boundary that separates one country from another.

Currency The money used in a country.

Cyclone A fierce tropical wind that forms at sea and blows into land in a spiral, bringing heavy rain. It often causes huge tidal waves on the coast.

Delta An area of land at the mouth of a river, formed by a build-up of soil and sand washed down by the river. These drop to the river bed when the river slows down as it nears the sea.

Embankment An artifically raised riverbank made to prevent flooding.

Hardcore Loose stones and other rubble used as the foundation underneath paved roads.

Irrigation A system of watering farmland, often by digging canals and ditches.

Jute A plant native to east India. The long, tough golden fibres of its leaves are used for making sacks, rugs, bags, mats and hammocks.

Literacy Being able to read and write.

Monsoon Seasonal winds which change direction from one time of year to another. In south-east Asia, the monsoon blowing in from the Indian Ocean brings heavy rains.

Polluted Damaged by chemicals, fumes or other waste products.

Population The number of people who live in one place.

Pulses The edible seeds of certain plants, such as lentils, peas and beans.

Slum An area of unplanned and overcrowded city housing, with no power, water supply, sewers or rubbish collection.

Staple A food that people eat every day.

Tributary A small river or stream that flows into a larger river.

Index

Page numbers in *italics* refer to entries in the fact box, on the map or in the glossary.